Young**writers**
— Est. 1991 —

GRIM TALES

Creative Capers

First published in Great Britain in 2025 by:

YoungWriters® Est. 1991

Young Writers
Remus House
Coltsfoot Drive
Peterborough
PE2 9BF
Telephone: 01733 890066
Website: www.youngwriters.co.uk

Foreword

Stories have the power to transport us – to other worlds, other times, and even into the minds of characters we may never meet in real life. But what happens when we take the stories we think we know and twist them into something unexpected? It was this idea that led to the creation of our latest competition for secondary school students: *Grim Tales*.

With the foundations of familiar tales as inspiration, these students had the confidence to let their originality and creativity shine brightly. The result is something remarkable   stories that will linger like the echoes of a forgotten legend.

Within this collection legends are rewritten, fairy tales unravel in surprising ways, and new myths are forged. You'll encounter heroes with dark secrets, villains seeking redemption, and endings that will leave you wondering long after you've turned the page.

Here at Young Writers it's our aim to inspire the next generation and instil a love of creative writing, and what better way to do that than for these young adults to see their work in print? The imagination and skill within these pages are proof that we are achieving that aim.

So, step into the shadows of *Grim Tales*, and prepare to see storytelling in a whole new light.

Contents

Engineering UTC Northern Lincolnshire, Scunthorpe

Sophia Morais Hadley (15)	58
Abeani Macdonald (15)	59
Elsie Thornton (15)	60

Haslingden High School & Sixth Form, Haslingden

Hermione Wormwell (12)	61
Freya Demetriou (12)	62
Reid Marsh (12)	63
Hayden Johnson (13)	64
Seb Wall (13)	65
Eris Farnworth (12)	66
Millie Peers-Holland (12)	67
Max Barlow (12)	68
Harry Rossiter (12)	69
Ben Hornby (13)	70
Charlie Altham (12)	71
Amelia Staines	72
Shahzana Mohammed	73
Rosemary Hodgetts (13)	74
George Hadfield (12)	75
Sam Mills (12)	76
Syd Larkin (13)	77

Kingsbridge Community College, Kingsbridge

Surayajith Ajith	78
Lexi Harris (12)	79
Eva Puncher (13)	80
Chloe Morris (13)	81
Chloe Jones (11)	82
Tilly Higgin (11)	83
Joshua Hine (12)	84

St Ives School, Higher Tregenna

Isla Brooks (14)	85
Max Vercesi (14)	86
Casey Ellsmore (14)	87
Sophie Murt (14)	88

Lucie Cole (16)	89
Henry James (14)	90
Macaulay John (14)	91
Phoebe Lennon (13)	92
Amy Timms (14)	93
Nevaeh Barnett (13)	94
James Davis (13)	95
Toby Stanbury (14)	96
Rhys Peters (13)	97
Oliver Deacon (14)	98

Thamesview School, Gravesend

Harrison Wright (15)	99

The Peterborough School, Peterborough

Alice Kovacs (14)	100
Ella Thomas (15)	101

The Royal Ballet School, Richmond Park

Toby McGowan (12)	102
Yoshino Harding (11)	103
Orla Warren (12)	104
Collins Rodrigues-Hesketh (11)	105
Milan Yep (12)	106
Charlie Waller (11)	107
Nylah Ali (12)	108
Tilly Thomas (13)	109
Frankie Keita (12)	110
Eliana Tse (13)	111
Felicity Ward (11)	112
Joseph Phillips (13)	113
Ned Phillips (12)	114
Uzziah Gray (12)	115
Rosie Zhang (11)	116
Arlo Hooper (12)	117
Yixin Zhou (12)	118
Ariella Assulin (11)	119
Oliver Quinn (11)	120

Torpoint Community College, Torpoint

Joe Tamblin (14)	121
Phoebe Danson (11)	122
Myrtille Gibbs (12)	123
Tristan Hill (12)	124
Freddie Shilton (12)	125
Mikey Bright (13)	126
Isla Symons-Goncalves (12)	127
Joe Davey (12)	128
Libby Weeks (12)	129
Aimee-Grace Ginger (13)	130
Nell Staniforth (13)	131
Isla-pearl Taylor (13)	132
Milo Smith (13)	133
Bessie Eastment (13)	134
Finn Kelly (14)	135
Joshua Toby (12)	136
Nevaeah Roberts (14)	137
Rhys Hulm (12)	138
Amelia Payne (11)	139

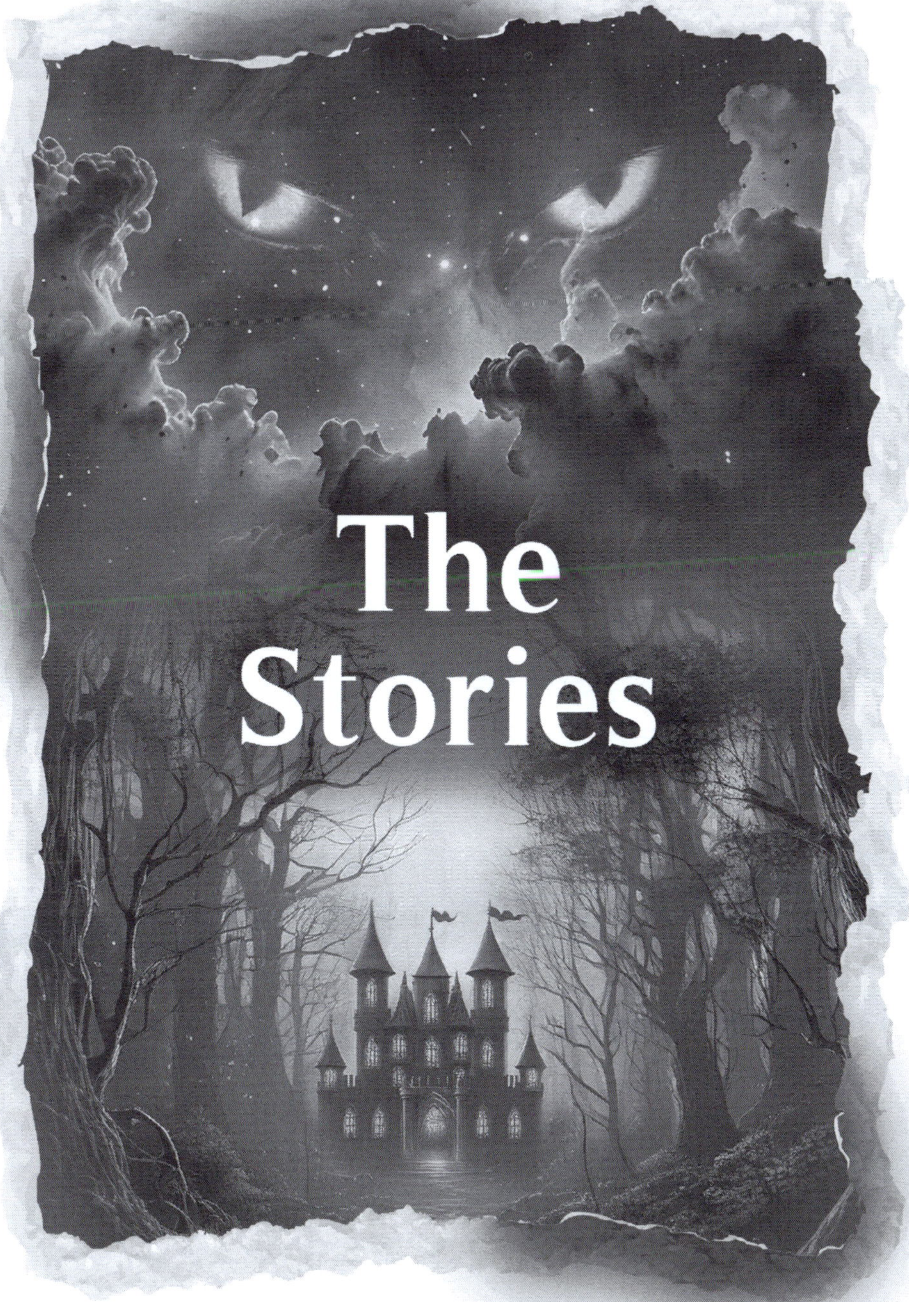
The
Stories

A Cindy Nightmare

The clock struck twelve. All that was heard next was a blood-curdling scream. The prince sprinted outside to a bloody glass slipper and bloody footprints going into the grim forest. The prince ran into the forest without hesitation.

Suddenly, the footsteps vanished. He looked down in despair. There were tyre tracks on the ground. He followed them until he heard a recognisable voice, the stepsisters torturing Cindy. Her ankle slit, her dainty hands had bones sticking out.

Out of pure rage, he launched at them, landing on a rock, killing everyone at the scene.

"Cindy, wake up, there are chores," a voice had called.

Tara Elshani (12)
Armadale Academy, Armadale

Untitled

Sally-Mae took cupcakes out of the oven, biting into one as the rest went in a basket. "Remember, don't take treats from others. There are vampires around here," her mother warned, as she left.
Sally skipped along the street, selling cakes to neighbours. A hand wiped the chocolate off her face. "You like chocolate?" asked the pale woman. Sally nodded, then she looked to see chocolate in the woman's hand. She hesitated before grabbing and biting into it.
The basket fell to the floor along with Sally-Mae. The woman sank her fangs into Sally's neck. Sally really should've listened.

Neive Williams (12)
Armadale Academy, Armadale

The New Girl

You may have heard of the tale of Cinderella, and how she moved away with a handsome fella. She left Stepmother alone with two evil stepsisters, forcing them to do housework, leaving them with blisters. Finally, they had had enough working in the basement. They decided they needed a replacement. A new girl arrived just a day after, bringing Stepmother close to happily ever after. Something was different, this girl wasn't normal, she was more rebellious than she ever was formal.

One day, the new girl must have gone insane. She probably just snapped as she shot them square in their evil brains.

Molly Donaldson (13)
Armadale Academy, Armadale

Mourning Sister

Stheno and Euryale were still mourning Medusa's death. Stheno wanted revenge... Bloodthirsty revenge. Euryale suggested asking Dionysus for wine to poison Poseidon. Surprisingly, he agreed. "I'll give you it," he said. "I heard what he did, and that's unforgettable." Stheno disguised herself as a priestess to enter Poseidon's temple. She had a smile on, a devious smile. She was being passive-aggressive, silently as she entered. "Poseidon, I brought you a drink."
As soon as he drank it, he felt faint and dropped like a fly.

Evie Fry (12)
Armadale Academy, Armadale

Sarah And Jaimie

Sarah and Jaimie wandered through the forest, their laughter echoing among the trees. As they strolled, they noticed an old treehouse hidden high above. Intrigued, they climbed up and stepped inside, only to be greeted by a strange flickering light.
Before they could react, the door slammed shut, and a voice boomed, "Welcome to my domain." A wizard appeared, trapping them in his enchanted home. Panic set as they realised escape would not be easy.
With the moonlight shining through the bars, Sarah saw a way out. Together, they gathered their courage and ran.

Hollie McLeish (13)
Armadale Academy, Armadale

The Red Shoes

It was a special Saturday, Amira's birthday. Her family sat around the living room, all holding gifts. Amira opened a bigger gift; there were red, sparkly shoes in a cardboard box. She became obsessed with them, wearing them to church, school, and everywhere. Amira noticed a change in them; they were harder to get off, as if they were tightening around her feet. One day after school, Amira was walking home when she suddenly started to dance in them. Her dancing continued as people passed by. She realised she was cursed... all because of being obsessed with some shoes.

Lena Kwiatkowska (13)
Armadale Academy, Armadale

Mrs Julie

Everyone adores little Mrs Julie, a sweet old grandma (or is she?) who invites children into her seemingly organised home. She loves baking so much that she bakes every day. What does she bake, you may wonder? Children...

Behind that broken mask is a corrupted hellhound driven by the taste and flavour of kids. Her twisted persona is obsessed with the bones and believes it is a crunchy delicacy you must enjoy. *Crunch, crunch.*

So children, no matter how warm or cosy it is inside, don't go in because what horror you see will shock your eyes.

Osatohanmwen Osamudiamen (12)

Armadale Academy, Armadale

Where's Jack?

Every day, Jack and Jill went up the hill to fetch a pail of water, but every day Jack would fall down and break his crown and Jill would come tumbling after. But Jill hated it when Jack tripped her up.

Today, Jill was acting strange. After Jack fell down and broke his crown, Jill lost it. She yelled at Jack and said to follow her into the woods. Hours later, Jill said to wait there and left.

Hours and days later, no return. Weeks after, a villager discovered Jack and took him back. But everyone was gone. How long was Jack really gone?

Ella Donaldson (12)
Armadale Academy, Armadale

Untitled

One day, I found out that the monster I had locked away for eternity had escaped. I soon found out the vampire had run to the village, claiming to be the lost princess. Of course, the villagers believed her, with her similarities to the king and queen.

I'd been trying to find ways into the village after the ban of magic users entering. One night, I heard screams from outside. I quickly ran to my window to see a figure running around the village. I ran to the village with a stake, and I rammed the stake through the vampire's chest.

Frankie McNaught (13)
Armadale Academy, Armadale

Little Red

I was going to help my sick, ailing grandmother, bringing her sweet treats. "Beware of the wolf!" my mother warned. But they didn't know the wolf liked me. As I skipped through the woods, I wasn't afraid. It was not a basket of treats that I carried, but rather a glimmering dagger.

Did you think I was the naive child, the little girl? I was the wolf in sheep's clothing, and when I ran home screaming, who do you think the townspeople believed? The big bad wolf or the innocent girl hidden behind a blood red hood?

Fraser Welsh (14)

Armadale Academy, Armadale

Highest Window Of Them All

There was a princess who lived up on top of a castle.
Her name was Princess Lola. Her mum and dad
wouldn't let her out of her room because of how
beautiful she was, blonde hair, blue eyes. She was
breathtaking, but her mum and dad were ginger with
brown eyes. They told everyone she'd passed away just
after she was born.

But the prince of Happy Land knew she was up there,
so one night, he snuck up into her bedroom and found
her. He said, "Everything will be fine," so they told
everyone. They all lived happily ever after.

Jessica Gallacher (12)
Armadale Academy, Armadale

The Monsters In Disguise

The hot sun shot beams of light upon the school. Our eyes shot to him. Tall and scaly, almost like a snake. As soon as their eyes met, he seemed as if everything poured out of his mind. He had fallen into a pool of love. After a while, they started hanging out often. Once they were watching TV, she dove in; she went for the bite, and he shoved her. "Hey!" They looked at each other in surprise. He wasn't a vampire? How? They had to escape; they flew away, knowing they had to find a new target. Somehow, somewhere, someday...

Megan Lee (12)
Armadale Academy, Armadale

Untitled

As the baby fox wanders through the woods, he catches sight of the frightening beast from the corner of his eye. The fox is the only one of his kind left, and he's wondering if he'll make it through the night. Bloodthirsty, the beast waits for its next tasty little fox. The brave hunter makes his way through the bushes and aims his gun at the beast. The little fox falls to the ground in agony, bleeding out on the grass.
The hunter realises his mistake as the beast approaches him from behind, and gobbles him right up.

Leilah McCourt (14)
Armadale Academy, Armadale

Is Magic Real?

Halloween, 1994. The last normal day. Since then, nobody had stepped foot outside. You didn't even hear cars driving across the motorway. Life became boring; nobody went in or came out. I hadn't even heard as little as a whisper, like I was the only person alive.
I decided to go outside. I walked out, and there weren't even birds flying around. I regretted going out. I ran back, the door wouldn't open, and I sat on the doorstep and wished the world would go back to normal.
Everything changed. Is magic real?

Hope Hutton (12)
Armadale Academy, Armadale

Untitled

Once upon a time, there were three little pig siblings who each built a house for themselves, one straw, one sticks, and one brick. But one day, a big, bad wolf came along who wanted to cause trouble.

So he destroyed the straw and the stick houses, but struggled initially with the brick one. So he took matters into his own hands and used his genius intelligence to turn the house to dust. He built a wrecking crane out of spare parts he found, drove it all the way up to the brick house, and... *Smash!* The house crumbled.

Liam Falconer (14)
Armadale Academy, Armadale

Devil's Curse

'You must pay the price' read the Ouija board. The man then screamed in pain as he shifted into a werewolf. The devil had cursed him, his eyes yellow as the sun, and fur brown like dirt, ears pointy like elf ears. His wife, hearing the screams, went down to check on him. "Hello? Is everything okay?" said the man's wife.
A growl came from the corner. She went over to the corner and, just like that, he pounced on her and ripped her in two from the waist.
The moral? Never play with a Ouija board.

Luke Leathem
Armadale Academy, Armadale

16

The Bear Family

One day, the bear family came across a house in the woods. They decided they liked the house and wanted it for themselves.

Straight away, Baby Bear ran to the kitchen where he saw a chair. Baby Bear tried to sit on the chair but he was too small. Mama Bear also tried to sit on the chair but was too big. Before Papa Bear could try and sit on the chair, someone came through the door, it was Goldie.

The bears attacked Goldie before cooking her for their tea. The bear family lived happily ever after in their new home.

Carrie Cowie (13)

Armadale Academy, Armadale

The Lady With Wings

There was once a lady with wings as bright as the sun. She looked like an angel. She was flying around and heard a little cry; it was a baby deer. She took it home to her little cabin and fed it some magic raspberries. The parents came looking for her, but she was gone. They didn't know that the lady with wings took it to help. The parents started worrying about what could have happened. They went back to the house, hoping she would come back; she did.

Moral of the story: don't leave anybody on their own.

Isabella Gracie (13)

Armadale Academy, Armadale

The Hated Child

Dressed in rags, this little girl was walking around with boxes on her feet. I felt so bad, then she walked slowly back to this shack-like house. I followed, I peeked through this old window. Her dad was screaming and hitting this girl. She was on the floor in tears, but I'd seen this happen before, but this time was different. She started hitting at her father. She had finally snapped. The father opened this chest filled with apples. *Crack!* His head got cut off by his now happy-looking daughter.

Millie McGillivray (12)
Armadale Academy, Armadale

Jack And The Loch Ness Monster

Once upon a time, a little boy named Jack went with his family to Loch Ness to go camping. Jack loved fishing, bait fishing. The biggest fish he caught was a 26lb carp. He brought his rod to Loch Ness hoping to catch a big fish.

They arrived at the lake and they set up their tent. Jack started fishing. He got a fish, but it was a bit unusual. It was really strong. He could see a sea monster.

He'd been on this fish for twenty minutes and he managed to reel it in. He caught the Loch Ness Monster.

Harry Clark (13)

Armadale Academy, Armadale

The Girl And The Old Woman

Once upon a time, there was a little girl. Her dream was to explore, but her father insisted it was too dangerous. But the girl didn't listen.
One day, she went out to the village without telling her father. After she arrived, she instantly felt off. She entered a building, but there was no one inside except for an old woman.
The girl asked her what was going on, but suddenly a trap door opened beneath her, and her father and everyone else who ever knew her never saw the poor little girl again.

Freddie Steel (12)
Armadale Academy, Armadale

Little Rattle

I waddle up to Lyla as her baby's gorgeous eyes peer up at me. They shimmer like the gold that saved her. "Give me my child!" I speak.

"No way!" she cries. I see the fear in her eyes. If the child says my name, he can go with his mother. "Little rattle," the baby cries.

My eyes widen in amazement, but I wake up with a scream. I wake up... next to my wife, Lyla. A whole lifetime I had lived was in the span of two hours.

Alexis Ige (12)
Armadale Academy, Armadale

Jack And The Beanstalk: Part Two

So, after Jack came down from his beanstalk with a harp then showed it to his mother, they thought they lived happily ever after. But the big guy woke up and saw his harp gone and came down from the beanstalk and soon broke into his mother's house to secure it. But when Jack came up, the big guy cut the beanstalk in half and went to the ground, and the harp was never stolen again.

Hamish Grant (13)
Armadale Academy, Armadale

The Pig's Mistake

I heard the stomps from the wolf. His huffs and puffs were loud, wind whistled through the house, making it wobble and creak. It kept growing stronger before eventually... it stopped. The wolf had given up!
I was overjoyed! I began to dance, not paying attention to anything. When I began to smell smoke, I realised my mistake, the wolf had only been trying to help...

Alexander King (13)
Armadale Academy, Armadale

Wings Of Vengeance

They fear a woman who wields power they cannot control. When the king betrayed her, stealing her wings, they cheered. When she cursed his daughter, they called her a monster.
But who was truly cruel? The woman who sought justice, or the men who sentenced her?

Rocio Thomson-Mombelli (14)
Armadale Academy, Armadale

The Downfall Of Cinderella

Cinderella finds the prince, but not for love. She's determined to return the glass slipper. She discovers he's a spellbound ruler. Disguised as an adviser, she overthrows the prince's enchantment.

When he learns her true identity, Cinderella has already claimed the throne. The prince, heartbroken and vengeful, curses her. Cinderella's rise to power shatters when the curse takes hold, as he makes her glass slippers scalding and unbearable for eternity. Cinderella screams in agony for help, and eventually dies of soreness and exhaustion.

The kingdom's people slowly lose hope as the prince continues to commit acts of unspeakable cruelty.

Sethumi Hennayake (12)
Denbigh High School, Denbigh

Peter's Broken Promise...

"Don't trust him, Robbie!" Emma's cries echo throughout Skull Rock. "Don't give him your heart. It won't save magic!"
"We're friends, remember?" I yell.
Silly boy... He has a powerful heart, yes. Will it save magic? No. When he dies, it will be me. I will be immortal.
I spot a dark green cloud. "Robbie, if you don't give me your heart now, the curse will kill us all." He did it. I beam with immortality.
I fly back to my sweet, sick Evelyn. "Love, you're saved!"
Cold hands... "No. I broke my promise..."
Neverland goes quiet and forever dark...

Millie Wynne-Price (14)
Denbigh High School, Denbigh

The Curse Of Deadfang Bay

This blood-curdling story starts with the infamous Captain Blackthorne and his crew setting sail through Deadfang Bay. A sea home to the dreaded Terrafin, a megalodon that feeds on the terror of passing pirates. They sailed for three days straight when on day three, a ghoul ship full of bloodthirsty death rattlers arose from the waters. The crew began returning fire at the ship.

Amidst the fight, an enormous figure, the Terrafin, erupted from the waters and crunched through the hull of the ship, sinking it and leaving Captain Blackthorne awaiting his death in the cold depths of Deadfang Bay.

Cai Jones (13)
Denbigh High School, Denbigh

Holiday From Hell

A man called Frankenstein had just come out of the travel agent after booking a holiday to Portugal. However, little did he know that it would be a holiday from hell.

It was the week before Portugal; Frankenstein received a message from an unknown number saying 'Enjoy Portugal and enjoy staying at Hotel Metropolitan.' He thought it was the hotel...

The day had arrived; Frankenstein got to the airport, got on the plane and arrived in sunny Portugal with his unknown friend. Frankenstein got to his room, and he got a message: 'Look outside.' There was a man with a weapon ready.

Max Bell (14)
Denbigh High School, Denbigh

Beauty And Literally The Beast

Once upon a time, there lived a beautiful belle and an astonishing beast. They were so happy together. Well, at least one was happy. The beast was clueless as to what was happening until Belle left her phone open next to him. The beast took a look at her phone and Belle was snapping Gaston.

The beast questioned her as it couldn't be anything serious, but Belle admitted that she was cheating. The beast was furious and ran to the kitchen, grabbed a big knife, crept up behind Belle, and stabbed her viciously.

Unlike other fairy tales, they didn't live happily ever after.

Izzy Williams (13)
Denbigh High School, Denbigh

The Last Visit Of Goldilocks

Goldilocks wandered into the bears' cottage, tired and hungry. She ate their porridge, broke their chairs, and fell asleep in Baby Bear's bed. But, as she slept, heavy footsteps creaked on the floor. The bears had returned. Their sharp teeth shone in the candles.

Scared, Goldilocks jumped up from the bed, but Papa Bear blocked the door. Mama Bear's claws scraped the wooden floor. Goldilocks tried to shout for help, but the sound was lost in terror.

By morning, the house was quiet once again. The only sign of her was a golden strand of hair, rough on the pillow.

Lewis Ashcroft (14)

Denbigh High School, Denbigh

The Start Of The Abnormal Apocalypse

It was just a normal school day for me, classes, messing around, just the usual... However, it didn't stay that way.

I had gone to the toilet during class. The bathrooms were eerily quiet and it felt deserted. How unusual... But I simply swept those thoughts under the carpet and went about my business.

This was where things changed. I left the bathroom. On my way back to the class, the lights were flickering and the atmosphere felt darker... and colder. I tried to ignore it but I turned around and saw a black figure chasing me...

"Anybody... Help me!"

Kitty Roberts (13)
Denbigh High School, Denbigh

The Swim Reaper

A shoal of fish were minding their own business when suddenly, the Swim Reaper appeared, a sinister orange and white fish, who had the intention to kill.
He swam upon the shoal and took a fish for ransom. His deal was to give a thousand grams of the finest seaweed or he would die.
The leader of the shoal, Gill, accepted the offer and got him his seaweed, although the Swim Reaper didn't know it was poisoned. He started eating it and after just three bites, his remains sank to the ocean floor. The ransomed fish was freed, and they lived happily ever after.

Kaiden Cluckie (13)
Denbigh High School, Denbigh

The Girl In Red

We walked through the forest, searching for prey.
There were footprints. We saw her, a young girl in red.
We retreated to the treeline and stalked her.
Snap! A twig under my paw broke. The girl called out,
"Who's there?" We stayed still, hoping she couldn't see
us. She continued to walk, we decided to make our
attack soon.
We got ready to pounce, the girl began to run and we
chased through the dark path. In the near distance,
there was a hut with a man in a red and white
checkered shirt and black jeans. He had an axe.
Whack!

Ray Thomas (14)
Denbigh High School, Denbigh

The Cursed Awakenings: Sleeping Beauty's Dark Reign

In a dark twist on the classic tale, Sleeping Beauty awakens, not as a gentle princess but as a vengeful villain. Cursed to sleep for a century, she cherishes resentment toward those who abandoned her.
The prince's kiss shatters the spell, but also her trust, leaving her with great power and a broken heart. Fuelled by rage, she turns against the kingdom that failed her, summoning dark magic to reclaim her throne.
No longer a damsel in distress, she becomes the nightmare of fairy tales, proving even the fairest of them all can become the most feared.

Sam Heyes (13)
Denbigh High School, Denbigh

The Mission Of The Seven Dwarfs

Once upon a time, there were seven dwarfs venturing high and far, when they found an island full of beauty. It was so flat, even the clumsiest person couldn't trip or fall.

The dwarfs went on expedition after expedition, finding new types of wood and flowers to decorate their houses. Soon, they would find out that their island was haunted by the spirits of the Evil Queen. Once they met back up, they would have to fight the spirits.

Luckily, they all survived their first night in their homes. Their only goal was to enter the Nether (a type of hell).

Lewys McCoombe (12)
Denbigh High School, Denbigh

Red's Fateful Day

Little Red Riding Hood was wandering through the forest on her way to her grandma's tiny cottage. Grandma was very, very ill, so Little Red was bringing biscuits and just going to give her company.
On the way, a bush started to shake; she thought nothing of it, but that was a mistake that she would regret. She continued strolling along, and out jumped a giant pack of grey wolves, and unfortunately, she got eaten, leaving only a pile of bones and three crumbs of biscuits.
Never walk through the forest by yourself, or the same might happen to you!

Iwan Ashcroft (14)
Denbigh High School, Denbigh

Blood All Over Her Hands

The sunset spread a red glow over the valley. Through the overgrown trees, a girl with a deep blood-red cloak skimmed through greenery with a dark plan in motion. The wolf smelled some uneasiness, and followed the girl. He hid in the wardrobe just before Little Red Riding Hood arrived. The wolf later came out, trying to save Grandma, but little did he know what was about to happen.

They were both found lying in puddles of blood, bloody handprints all over the walls. Hiding deep in the forest, Little Red Riding Hood started planning her next move.

Catherine Williams (13)
Denbigh High School, Denbigh

The Poisoned Prince

Snow White lay there dead, encased in glass, as I approached. Her beautiful face, paler than usual. The seven dwarfs stood around. I lifted the glass and bent down to kiss her. Our true love's kiss.

I could taste an apple, the poisoned apple. I started to choke, vomit rising up my throat, my body went numb, and I collapsed. I was dying. The poisoned vomit started infecting the grass, leaving it dead in its wake. I heard the dwarfs screaming as they attempted to run away. I heard their screams until I heard nothing at all. Until I died.

Macey Bowers (13)
Denbigh High School, Denbigh

The Starving Boy

In a poor village, a starving boy found an apple on the floor. He took it home, but his parents demanded more.

The next night, he returned and found a mysterious old pensioner who offered him a sack of apples if he never spoke again. The boy agreed. Rich beyond, his parents feasted, but when they mocked his silence, he tried to protest. At once, his mouth vanished.

Desperate, his parents dragged him to the woods, but the old man was gone. That night, they chided a spirit, and the boy, voiceless and alone, wandered into the dark.

Alfie Parry (13)
Denbigh High School, Denbigh

A Hellish Nightmare

One glorious evening, eight little Smurfs were adventuring through the deep depths of hell. These Smurfs clawed their way up the mountains upon mountains of corpses and saw an ocean of lava.
This scared the Smurfs because they were trapped in hell, but one of the Smurfs plucked up the courage to float across on a rotting corpse but ended up stuck, so they hatched another plan to make stepping skulls for him to hop back on over.
This took so long that it was nearly supper time so they used mythical capes to fly all the way home.

Noah Parry (13)
Denbigh High School, Denbigh

Just Perfect

It was a dark night. We slowly approached the cottage. I was nervous, but everyone assured me it was okay. We entered and went to find the first meal. We knew there were three, and this was the first. We all devoured it, but agreed it was too tough. The second one tasted great, but there wasn't much there to eat. The final one looked amazing - you could even say it was just perfect.

It was a girl named Goldilocks. She seemed familiar, but it didn't matter; it was a delicious meal. So baby bear's hunt was successful.

Sam Garvey (13)
Denbigh High School, Denbigh

The Evil Tooth Fairy

A young girl knocked out her teeth. She was afraid. Across her school, there was a joke going around about a tooth fairy that robs your money and teeth. The school bell rang. It was home time.

The young girl ran home like a rocket, and once home, hid the fallen teeth. For the next two hours, she booby trapped her room, to wake her up if there was motion. The time was 9pm, the girl's bedtime. She was fast asleep until... *Squeak!* echoed throughout the house. She awoke to a fairy flying out of her window.

Lucas Roberts (13)
Denbigh High School, Denbigh

Cry Of The Cold

In every fairy tale, every princess gets their happily ever after. Not me. Growing up, I was told I had great power, a true prodigy; everyone called it a dream. I'd compare it to a curse.

My biggest regret is what I did to my sister. I couldn't control it. She got shot in the heart with ice. Worst of all, I was the one who ended her life even after she sacrificed herself for me. Her cold, isolated, distant sister.

As she stood there frozen in time, I felt distraught and so heartbroken. I could never go back.

Seren Williams (13)
Denbigh High School, Denbigh

Little Red Riding Hood

One day, a small child is ready to leave her home to deliver goods to her grandmother, but is advised to walk on the main path. On her way, she is stopped by a wolf, and she tells the wolf where she is going, to her grandmother's house. The wolf arrives at her grandmother's house to trick her.
She is tricked, but with one quick strike, she slays the big bad wolf and saves her grandmother. She returns home and tells great tales of her victory, till she grows old with time and requests goods from her granddaughter.

Gethin Jones (14)
Denbigh High School, Denbigh

The First And Last Day

It was Sarah's first day at her new high school. She was sitting in her science lesson when two kids came to sit with her throughout the lesson. Sarah became friends with them, and they decided that they should hang out after school.

As the day went on, Sarah grew to know them more, but little did Sarah know that this would be a terrible mistake, and this mistake would cost her a long and torturous death.

The next day, Sarah was found in a forest with her heart torn out. And the two kids she was with? Vanished.

Paige Mactaggart (14)
Denbigh High School, Denbigh

Untitled

In the kingdom of Arendelle, Prince Hans saw Queen Elsa's magic unleash an eternal winter, putting everyone in danger. He tried to stop her, but Elsa refused to listen, lost in her powers. Anna, Elsa's sister, believed Elsa's lies and turned against Hans.
To save the kingdom, Hans led the people to confront Elsa. In a final battle, he broke her icy spell and freed Arendelle, but Elsa and Anna painted Hans as the villain, and he was exiled. Hans vowed to return for the true villain, who wears a crown of ice.

Upunya Gurusingha (14)
Denbigh High School, Denbigh

The Queen Of Broken Hearts

He used to shout at me for hours, fury etched into every line on his face. I would shuffle my playing cards as he spat insults. I had stopped calling him my father many years ago. After all, he wasn't deserving of the title. I used to dream of him being a loving parent. Now I only dreamed of revenge.

Now, looking down at his bloody face, I feel a great sense of power as I plunge the sword through his heart. I catch sight of the card, spattered with scarlet in my fist. The Queen of Hearts. I smile.

Eva Wynne (13)
Denbigh High School, Denbigh

The Three Murdering Pigs

The three little pigs were on a walk and found a nice farm with a supply of carrots. They decided to look further to see if there was any more. There wasn't. They headed back home to grab a bag and a few buckets.

Once they arrived home, they began to search; however, they were missing. One pig turned to see a wolf, but he wasn't mad. The wolf was making the house bigger. He stayed silent until the rest saw. The other pigs saw and got mad, so they chased him to a forest and murdered him.

Finley Hayes (14)
Denbigh High School, Denbigh

The Three Little Piggies

My two brothers and I were fixing a straw house when a wolf challenged us to a boxing match, where each of us fought a round.

On the day of the match, my brother was ready, saying he would go first. He was knocked out in one punch. Now, my other brother and I were scared, but we continued. After my brother's round, the wolf was weak, so it was time for me to go.

After a tense round, I found his weak spot - an uppercut. Soon, he was on the floor, knocked out cold. We actually beat him.

Jac Morley Moore (14)
Denbigh High School, Denbigh

Little Red

There once was a girl who loved to read, her name was Little Red. She had always loved books and you would never see her without a book. When she would cook, she would use a book and whenever you would look, she would have a book.

One day, she went to the woods of course. She took a book but when it turned to night, she hadn't returned and when her parents went to look, all they could find was Little Red's book.

Alfie Wedge
Denbigh High School, Denbigh

Snow White And The Seven Deadly Sins

Once upon a time, there was a princess - Snow White. She *prided* herself on her looks, gloating to her evil stepmother, who became *envious* and ordered Snow White's murder.

The princess used the hunter's *lust* to her advantage, offering him a kiss in return for freedom. Upon hearing this, the queen, filled with *wrath*, decided to murder the princess herself.

Snow White was too *lazy* to seek help, so she sat on a rock and sang to the birds. The disguised queen offered Snow White poisoned apples. Overcome by *greed*, she ate them all, dying at her stepmother's feet.

Kalista Senaratne-Niland (17)
Devonport High School For Girls, Peverell

The Enchanted Flour Bag

In a distant kingdom, a beautiful baker named Emily discovered an enchanted flour bag.
One morning, she used it to bake bread that came to life, each loaf singing merry tunes. The villagers were amazed, however the corrupted king demanded magical bread for himself. When he tried to take them, they simply danced away, spreading joy everywhere. Emily's bakery became famous, and the king, tired of chasing bread, admitted defeat. Emily shared her secret with him: kindness made the flour magical.
All of the kingdom thrived on Emily's enchanted bread, and the once-cruel king became a benevolent ruler.

Lilly-Ruth Robertshaw (12)
Devonport High School For Girls, Peverell

Awakening

Sleeping Beauty doesn't wake to love's kiss; she wakes to different time periods, slipping between centuries as reality decays around her. Castles crumble, loved ones vanish, and eerie voices whisper in the dark. Each awakening is worse than the last.

She soon learns the truth: the curse wasn't meant to keep her asleep; it was meant to keep something inside her contained. Every kiss weakens the seal, and the final one will unleash an ancient horror.

Now she must choose: stay asleep forever, or break the cycle before the dark curse dooms the world. But... what if the monster is her?

Isla Soper (14)
Devonport High School For Girls, Peverell

Luna The Nature Wolf

Once upon a time, there was a wolf called Luna. Every night, Luna would go out and howl. However, when Luna howled, plants would grow and thrive, whilst her fur glowed silver in the moonlight.

But one day, some nasty humans came and captured Luna for her power. Luna lay silent in her cage and refused to howl. The humans got annoyed and refused to feed her. But they forgot to lock the door of the cage, so Luna got out.

She returned home and nature was restored. Luna never got captured again. She howled forevermore.

Lowena Powell-Jones (13)
Devonport High School For Girls, Peverell

The Girl In Red

I ran. Ran because my life depended on it. My basket was long gone, but it didn't matter. All that did was that I made it out alive.

My hair blocked my vision in streaks of chestnut. My mind whirred. My crimson cape slipped down, but I didn't care. The howling seemed to fade, or it was in my head.

I slowed. It truly was quieter. I looked around. The trees seemed to stare at me tauntingly. I breathed heavily. Then it hit me. I was lost. Being chased by a wolf. And my life depended on finding my way...

Maya Kmito (12)
Devonport High School For Girls, Peverell

The Last Petal

The second-to-last petal fell to the ground. Belle knew what she had to do, almost as if she had lived this night before. Belle leapt down the stairs searching for the beast. He sat in the corner looking like he had been crying. She crept over to him.
The last petal began to fall. She leaned in for a kiss, swiping against his cheek. The petal hit the ground. The beast was still a beast.
Belle began to feel light-headed and fell to the floor. Was this all a dream, a trick, or was it the truth?

Meredith Holdstock (12)
Devonport High School For Girls, Peverell

The Starlight Merchant

Marrow arrived at dusk, his cart rattling over cobblestones, the scent of candlewax and decay clinging to him. Jars swathed in midnight velvet lined his stall, each promising bottled starlight, one wish granted with the turn of a lid. The villagers, hollow-eyed and despondent, gathered, their hopes fragile as gossamer.

Eloise, resentful of her ordinary life, eagerly proceeded, her gaze sharp with hunger. She twisted the lid, and a silver mist unfurled, forming a thin shimmering door. Without hesitation, she stepped through.

The door slammed shut. Marrow, already fading, murmured, "To covet what is not yours, invites consequence beyond comprehension."

Sophia Morais Hadley (15)
Engineering UTC Northern Lincolnshire, Scunthorpe

Plastic Golden Idols

My village - a place of simple joys and loving smiles - reduced to smouldering dust and broken souls. I stumbled from the rubble of my family shop, clutching my arm, resolutely ignoring the bile climbing my throat at the sight of my bone piercing through my skin. Screaming, crying, begging for help. Five of them should be plenty, surely they'd send help.
Relief flooded my veins at the sight of them coming closer, only to vanish as I was shoved aside, unimportant and invisible to the saviours of the world. I swore that day that I would never be a hero.

Abeani Macdonald (15)
Engineering UTC Northern Lincolnshire, Scunthorpe

A Secret Is Revealed

I rummaged around the room, looking for anything that seemed even remotely out of place. Then I saw it. A book that stuck out more than the rest.

I picked it up, and it was heavy. I opened it, and there were no pages inside. Just a metal door with a lock embedded. I had already found a key, it was hidden under the rug.

I sprinted to it and unlocked the box. Too late to think about what I might be uncovering, I opened the box and found a letter addressed to my dad, from after he died...

Elsie Thornton (15)

Engineering UTC Northern Lincolnshire, Scunthorpe

Revenge

On the edge of a lonely rock, a saddened widow lived. Her wiry hair waved gently down and her moon-like eyes poised in the gloom. Something about her just seemed strange; the villagers stayed well away from the woman and accused her of doing voodoo. Despite her numerous quirks, she desperately longed for a child.

Miraculously, she had a daughter. She loved her unconditionally, but the villagers thought she wasn't worthy of such a significant responsibility, and the king confirmed this. So one night, guards took the child, never permitting her to meet her mother.

She sobbed, devastated. She plotted an evil plan to get back at the king.

Hermione Wormwell (12)
Haslingden High School & Sixth Form, Haslingden

Back There Again

It's been years since I've been out there. Nobody believed me, but it's real. Wonderland.

Today's the day that I leave this place. I've planned it for so long, being their version of normal for months, so that they finally discharge me. But I'm not. I have had dreams about that place. Wonderland. It has to be real.

This is when they finally come and get me, the nurses. They're releasing me, finally. I'm free. But it's been so long.

I'm outside. There it is: the rabbit hole. It's like it's magnetic. I walk towards it and I'm back there again.

Freya Demetriou (12)
Haslingden High School & Sixth Form, Haslingden

Demons

One day, all the people in the world were struck by a wave of anxiety engulfing the world and making people go to shambles. Every single person could see things. No one could see before monsters, horrific creatures, came from the shadows.

But then a silence was held. For a while, there was no noise until a banjo struck. Then, all of a sudden, doors. Japanese doors opened from underneath them, and they were transported to another world. The demon realm, where it went on forever, with Japanese yokai and demons that came and slaughtered people in gruesome ways. Billions dead.

Reid Marsh (12)

Haslingden High School & Sixth Form, Haslingden

The Bagpiper

Deep in the glens of Scotland lies the phantom piper who plays on stormy nights where the wind grows fierce and the waves crash hard.

Beatrice stood at the mouth of the cave, phone in hand. She talked to her fans, who had dared her to visit the caves of Duntrune Castle to discover the piper who petrified the fiercest of men.

She didn't believe in stories, why should she? It was all fantasy to lecture people. Likes spewing out onto her phone, she entered determinedly.

For passersby, she had vanished into the dark, following the noise of the shrill bagpipes...

Hayden Johnson (13)
Haslingden High School & Sixth Form, Haslingden

Don't Change

In Midville High lived an average school boy. He didn't have many friends and was known only as the weird kid, he wanted that to change.

So, one misty night, he said his wish, which was to be a popular boy, just as a shooting star went by. He didn't think much of it until he went to school. Everyone was surrounding him like he was a different person. It wasn't until he looked in the mirror and realised he was a different person. He was now the captain of the school football team.

Then, all of a sudden, he was stuck in the multiverse.

Seb Wall (13)
Haslingden High School & Sixth Form, Haslingden

Off With Their Heads

It was a fun, lively day in Wonderland where everyone was chatting and dancing and laughing - until that girl arrived here in Wonderland. For the first few days, she didn't really speak. Until she made friends with everyone, that took my popularity away from me.
I. Was. Furious. The girl, who introduced herself as Alice, came up to me one day, smiling eerily ear to ear. She held out a red, heart-shaped box. I was confused, why was she giving me this? Was it a trap? Was she being nice?
I hesitantly grabbed the box, opening it... and inside...

Eris Farnworth (12)
Haslingden High School & Sixth Form, Haslingden

The Hole That Killed

After Belle and the Beast got married, it was nice for two years. They lived nicely and happily, but one year later, they were going for a walk through the forest. Belle dropped something, not realising she had.
Five minutes later, she realised. She told the Beast she would go get it, and he waited. She went to find it but fell into a hole in the ground. In the ground, she didn't even shout for help because she fainted. The Beast went to look for her, but failed.
A few days later, he was told she had died. A year later, he was still upset.

Millie Peers-Holland (12)
Haslingden High School & Sixth Form, Haslingden

The Mushroom

Dorothy drifted on the yellow brick. Later, she saw a scarecrow having its hay taken out as the sound of a razor was heard, making her hair fall out.

After a while, Dorothy saw a Tin Man standing still and he started to beep. So she grabbed WD-40 and sprayed it on his joints, and walked off while the sound of wheels followed behind.

After a while, Dorothy saw a lion's stuffing fall out, so she ran and hugged the lion tightly as a nurse-like figure came from the sky, taking him away.

The dream had ended and the light brought her up.

Max Barlow (12)
Haslingden High School & Sixth Form, Haslingden

The Urban Monster

Once, there was an urban explorer who found an abandoned mansion in Manchester. Once he got there, he was trying to find a way in. He tried a window and climbed in. He got in and started exploring and taking pictures.

He then heard deep breathing nearby. When he opened the door, there was a curtain with a silhouette behind. He moved the curtain and screamed when he saw a monster made of knives in front of him. As he was about to run, the monster chopped his arms, then legs, then his head.

The police never knew what happened.

Harry Rossiter (12)

Haslingden High School & Sixth Form, Haslingden

Freakenstein

Deep in the depths of Bury, Ramsbottom, Johnathan is thinking about Gorilla Sofa when a note is slipped under his door. He picks up and reads the note, it says: 'Gathering Volunteers For Experiment'.
He calls the number on the back of the note, and they tell him his appearance is going to be altered. He thinks nothing of it.
He goes to the location provided and they strap him to a table. Electricity flows through his body and the scientists attach parts to him. He is turned into a freak, a freak called Freakenstein.

Ben Hornby (13)
Haslingden High School & Sixth Form, Haslingden

The Troll And The Golden Child

Once upon a time, there was a child with a magical golden amulet. The child was loved by everybody but one troll. The troll had one goal: to rule the kingdom, but the one person who could stop him from doing that was the golden child with magical powers. So the troll kidnapped him and with no one to defend the kingdom, the troll took control of the kingdom.

However, one of the troll's advisors knew this was wrong and he planned to release the amulet's power. One night, the advisor found and released the child. Freedom!

Charlie Altham (12)
Haslingden High School & Sixth Form, Haslingden

Beautiful But Not For Long

Once upon a time, there was a young girl. She had beautiful blonde hair and was very intelligent. She lived in a beautiful house, but it wouldn't be beautiful forever.

She was a lovely girl in school, and all her teachers said she was a charm to each, but one day she came home to see that her house was taken over by insects, but not normal insects. They could talk! Her parents didn't know as they worked late. She tried to get them out, but had no luck.

When her parents came home, they were not happy at all.

Amelia Staines
Haslingden High School & Sixth Form, Haslingden

Untitled

My friend was taken from me, I have no idea where she is. She is lost. I can't find her. I'm worried. I looked everywhere and asked everyone, but no one could find her and she left a note asking for help. I hope I can find her. She can't have gone far, could she?
I'm in a dark room surrounded by people, and not knowing what to do. Do I go find her? Well, obviously, what am I thinking? I'm definitely going to find her. She is my best friend. I am not gonna leave her out there scared.

Shahzana Mohammed
Haslingden High School & Sixth Form, Haslingden

The Fight

I put on my shining armour and unsheathed my silver sword, still stained crimson from the last battle. As I marched out into the burning sunlight, I noticed the soldiers who would fight alongside me. I was sure we could win this.

I took the first step towards the emerald coloured dragon before I plunged my sword into its scaly side and it roared in pain. I smiled. The soldiers descended upon the thing until at last someone held up its heart and climbed upon its still body.

We had won.

Rosemary Hodgetts (13)
Haslingden High School & Sixth Form, Haslingden

What Happened To The Old Man?

It started when a man was hiking in the dark, long woods in the middle of the day. He was having a great time, striding up long mountains and running back down them while being hit violently by the wind.
Out of nowhere, a 14-year-old boy stood upon the long mountain which the man was hiking.
When he got to the top the boy was friendly and he had some food and shared it with him. Until the boy led the man to the very top of the mountain. Then out of nowhere, pushed him off the cliff.

George Hadfield (12)
Haslingden High School & Sixth Form, Haslingden

Untitled

After Goldilocks ran away from the bears in the forest, she heard a twig snap. It was Papa Bear, hunting her down. She started to run as fast as she could, but she could hear him getting closer and closer.

All of a sudden, she saw a cave and she then jumped into the shadows of the cave to try and hide. Papa Bear stood at the edge of the cave. He stood there, staring into the shadows.

Luckily, he ran back into the forest and somehow, Goldilocks escaped the three bears once again.

Sam Mills (12)

Haslingden High School & Sixth Form, Haslingden

The Near Stabbing At The Holiday Home

I was camping with my dad, and there was an abandoned holiday home by us. On the first day, I was curious, so I had a look around the outside of the house and saw a broken window. So I had a look in and saw some things in it. But the next day, I went inside the house and heard something fall from upstairs, so I looked and I looked in every room.
In one room, there was a guy and he turned and he started chasing me with a knife and I ran down and out the window.

Syd Larkin (13)
Haslingden High School & Sixth Form, Haslingden

The Three Fairies

The king ordered, "Whoever finds my child, they get all my wealth."
"We will find him!"
"Who said that?"
"We are the three fairies."
The king said, "Okay, then you may begin."
Bonnie said, "Let's begin the search."
They flew through the evil forest. Bonnie said, "I can't believe it! I got the map to the evil maze!"
Fasto said, "Here we are at the evil maze."
Evan said, "I will lead you to the maze. I think we can fly through the maze.
Bonnie said, "Let's go."
Suddenly, they stopped flying. Evan stopped, and they stopped moving.

Surayajith Ajith
Kingsbridge Community College, Kingsbridge

Insanity

Another late shift. I hate having to walk through the woods so late. It's almost like the whole atmosphere changes when I walk through here. And there's always this deathly screaming, but this time, it feels different. It's like it's following me, getting louder.
I start to run, but I can't escape it. It won't stop.
You thought the story ended once you finished reading, didn't you? Idiot. You know, the whole time I've been trying to escape this monster when I should be escaping myself, everything. Please. Help.
It will always follow you. You will never escape it. Never.

Lexi Harris (12)
Kingsbridge Community College, Kingsbridge

The Kraken

A fearsome creature, feared throughout the seven seas by pirates and sailors alike. But have you heard the true story?

Long ago, the kraken was given a job by the King of Atlantis, as it sank, to protect the ancient city from the outside world, until such time came that they were ready to accept such power. On the king's dying breath, the kraken swore to protect Atlantis.

For years, the kraken had sunk ships and claimed many sailors' lives. But only because they invaded his home and threatened his kingdom. So the kraken was feared forevermore!

Eva Puncher (13)
Kingsbridge Community College, Kingsbridge

Peter Hook

I stare at Peter for what feels like an eternity, desperately willing for him to understand. He stares back, his green eyes cold and unforgiving. He thinks I'm evil, a murderer. But he can't kill me, he can't, else he'll never know.

"Walk the plank," he says. The boys behind him begin to chant, and whatever hope I had left of getting through to my son drains away. I step backwards until I reach the end of the plank and look back at Peter.

I was the first thing he saw in the world, and now he'll be my last.

Chloe Morris (13)
Kingsbridge Community College, Kingsbridge

Blood Moon

A shrill scream pierced the night sky. The deed was done. The curse had struck again. Everyone in the small village rushed to the source of the noise. Out of the door came a mother holding the lifeless body of a young boy.

I looked into the sky. The moon shone above, casting a red glow on us all.

Every blood moon, at midnight exactly, a curse claims a life. This child must be loved by all. If there are no children left, it will haunt a family until they bear one. Then it will die the day it is born.

Chloe Jones (11)

Kingsbridge Community College, Kingsbridge

The Ghost House

I woke up. I was a bit confused at first. I was somewhere that I had never been before. The grass grew in clumps, and the flowers were all a grey-blue sort of colour. The wind blew hard on my face.
I got up off the ground and saw a house in front of me. It had never been there before! I started to walk towards the white ghostly house.
Five minutes later, I was in the house. It was cold and damp, so I decided to light a fire.
As I got the match, I saw a black figure.

Tilly Higgin (11)
Kingsbridge Community College, Kingsbridge

The Death Troll

Once upon a time, there was a man who went to a bridge and saw something under it. He went to investigate and saw a sleeping troll so he slowly started to walk away but stepped on a stick and woke the troll and got him very angry.
The troll ripped off his arms and legs so he couldn't do anything and threw him into a river. Then cleaned his hands from the blood. Then the splatters of blood. Then went back to sleep.
I slowly walked over the bridge and then I ran.

Joshua Hine (12)
Kingsbridge Community College, Kingsbridge

The Murder Of King Duncan

I gazed out the window at the ominous forest below: wind whispering the secrets of the sinners. The air started picking up mist as the owls shrieked. My heart pounded. Mist turned to heavy rain, drenching everything. My sweat-soaked hands started to turn red. I frantically rubbed my palms together, trying to escape the permanent witness of my immoral actions. I ran to the bathroom to wash the guilt from my conscience.

I walked back and glanced out the window again. The rain was hammering as lightning struck the lake like the everlasting pain of living with extreme regrets.

Isla Brooks (14)
St Ives School, Higher Tregenna

Creative Writing: Grim Tale!

Creative writing is a villain. It lurks in the nooks and crannies of literature. Every English class is poisoned with this dark omen of writing with your imagination. I was forced to write this horrible tale. A tale so true that it will send shivers down your spine.

Reading is culpable, inferring is complicated; but creative writing is a villain. Creative art is mesmerising, creative music is magical, but creative writing, creative writing is a villain, the villain.

Why did I write this story? To warn you about all the dangers of creative writing. Creative writing is evil.

Max Vercesi (14)

St Ives School, Higher Tregenna

Child Aspiring

In a car, going to Redruth from St Ives, Cindy was telling her dad about how she wanted to be a linguist and that she was already learning German. She seemed incredibly knowledgeable and passionate about this career, and she had even taken her school options to suit the job.

Sadly, her dad didn't think too highly of the idea and said, quote, "I don't want to be mean, but you should focus on an actual trade, rather than that - but never do building."

Cindy was fourteen and apparently not allowed to dream. All of us are allowed to dream.

Casey Ellsmore (14)

St Ives School, Higher Tregenna

Blurring

In the shadows of St Ives, a figure cloaked in darkness plotted revenge. Known only as the Phantom, he was once a brilliant inventor, betrayed by those he trusted. Fuelled by anger, he crafted a device capable of plunging the town into eternal night.

As the sun set, he unleashed his creation, casting a veil of darkness over the streets. Panic ensued; the townsfolk stumbled in fear. But deep within, the Phantom felt a flicker of doubt. Was he truly a villain, or just a soul seeking justice? In that moment, the line between hero and monster blurred into one.

Sophie Murt (14)
St Ives School, Higher Tregenna

Siren

They warned me about your song: a methodical symphony that invades the mind and floods one's introspection long enough to drag a sailor to their death. The last thing their filtered vision perceives is the uncanny valley of a scaled hand hidden beneath falsified flesh.

When I prepared to set sail to uncharted expanses of waves, they gazed upon me like I was the living dead. Like my fate had been sealed. Like all that would remain of my existence would be discarded bone, floating in the abyss of the sea. But you wouldn't do that. Not to me. Right?

Lucie Cole (16)
St Ives School, Higher Tregenna

Guilt

I am standing in my castle, looking out into a dark hole. Not even the mighty walls can protect King Duncan from his death.

This guilt is burning inside me, like a fierce woodland fire. The air is cold and breathless. Crows circle above the castle tower and sit to rest. The sun is setting behind the monstrous hills, and tall branches stretch high like daggers, haunting me. The wind is getting stronger and howls like an animal in pain.

Will all great Neptune's ocean wash this blood clean from my hand? Shall I own up? What did I do?

Henry James (14)
St Ives School, Higher Tregenna

The Talisman

After a drawn-out day at work in the hustle and bustle of downtown Manchester in 1979, Eliza finds herself in the locker room of the department store where she works. It's just her, but a pulsating red light burdens her mind, so she goes to see what it is.

It's a rune of some sort, and it has three strikes on its face. Eliza stuffs it into her bag and takes it home for further investigation and analysis.

She forgets about the rune, but it's still there, and it's taking notes about her life and her style of living.

Macaulay John (14)

St Ives School, Higher Tregenna

The Chill

As I stand looking out the window, the cold air nips at my face and brushes over my fair skin. The night feels dimmer than usual: it sends a chill down my spine, which makes me shudder. My eyes dart around at the familiar surroundings, trying to make me feel a sense of comfort, but nothing.
Had our plan really worked out? Was our future secured? Were we really about to get away with this? I quickly snap out of it and reassure myself that it will all absolutely be okay. We had succeeded with our plan to kill him...

Phoebe Lennon (13)

St Ives School, Higher Tregenna

The Owl In The Darkness

I walked along the cold, decaying floor with bloodied, shaking palms. The hollow, dark night expanded before me, and dark figures swayed in and out of tangled branches. A frost-bitten wind crawled around my numb spine.

In the dense treetops, an owl's hoot escaped and echoed around in the silence. Beady, amber eyes burned into my skull, and I couldn't hide the terrifying thought of how alike they looked to Puncan's. The guilt of what I had done sat heavy and unmoving in the pit of my stomach, forever there.

Amy Timms (14)
St Ives School, Higher Tregenna

Downfall

It's everywhere! All over the news. Everyone knows about it. A deadly virus called Cietric has affected the world drastically. Once you get it, there is no saving you. You slowly turn into a dark beast with no control over your actions.

All everyone wants is for it to end or for a cure to be made, but that is not possible for a long time because all of the scientists have been turned, leaving me and a few survivors. I have to start what ended. Their dreams were crushed but not mine. I have to survive this...

Nevaeh Barnett (13)
St Ives School, Higher Tregenna

A Deadly Curse

There once was a curse set all over Europe, and it was starting to spread over all of the UK, Wales, Scotland, Ireland and Northern Ireland. Soon, it got near Scotland and the people tried their best to push the curse back and drive it back to where it came from and back to the people who sent the curse in the first place. It was a really annoying curse which was sent by the north of the USA by Canada, Russia, Ukraine, Romania and Georgia, who helped put this deadly curse over the southwest part of England.

James Davis (13)
St Ives School, Higher Tregenna

The Dark Abyss

I stared down into the dark abyss from the castle, the moon glistening in the dark sky. I saw a dark figure in the courtyard from the corner of my eye. He had no shoes on and ripped-up clothes. As I got a more focused look, he had a huge gash on his head, with blood pouring down his face.

No way - it can't be! It was Banquo! *But I thought I had killed him - twenty stab wounds in his head! There is no way he could have survived that! I must be going crazy!* I froze in fear...

Toby Stanbury (14)
St Ives School, Higher Tregenna

My Name

The world called me a monster, but I was only ever a man who refused to kneel. They stole my name, my family, my life, left me with nothing but vengeance. So I took everything from them.

Their king was first, his crown melting in my hands as his palace burned. The heroes came next, one by one, their legacy crumbling beneath the weight of my fury. Now they whisper my name in fear, the same way I whispered for mercy. But mercy is for the weak, and I am not weak. Not anymore, and never again.

Rhys Peters (13)
St Ives School, Higher Tregenna

Ghost!

As I looked out of my balcony, I saw a figure which I recognised, so I looked closer and it was my best friend, but in a ghost form. I was in shock! Had he been killed, or was I dreaming?

He started to talk about when we went out together, and then he flew away from me and said, "Don't be jealous or greedy - trust me!"

I replied with, "I won't be. Thank you. Talk to you again soon." Then, my mate came up to me, but all I was doing was thinking.

Oliver Deacon (14)

St Ives School, Higher Tregenna

Cinderella: From The Perspective Of A Random Panda Named Bob

I was watching the ball from the ajar entrance, when Cinderella burst out, apparently very stressed. I saw her drop one of her shoes, which her dance partner picked up.

I spoke, "What happened there?"

"She's gone!" he cried. "I can't find her!"

I watched her continue to run away, stupefied at his royal idiocy. "She's right there!" I hollered at him. He got the idea and followed her helplessly, leaving the odd glass footwear behind.

I decided to hop into it and began bouncing after Charming. Why did I do that? Why not? This book doesn't make sense anyway!

Harrison Wright (15)

Thamesview School, Gravesend

Golden No More

Rapunzel knelt beside me - tears streamed down her face. "You were my new dream... but dreams don't last forever," she whispered.

I thought, just for a second, *I can't let Mother Gothel have you*. My fingers curled around the glass shard. My hand grasped her hair. She gasped as the glass slid across her throat. Blood spilt down her dress. She choked, her eyes wide with betrayal. Her once gleaming gold hair dulled as her magic faded. She slumped backwards, her eyes rolled back into her head. Our story never ended in freedom - only disloyalty and sorrow.

Alice Kovacs (14)

The Peterborough School, Peterborough

Forever Thorns

Once upon a time, Aurora was no fairy tale princess. As a child, she set forests ablaze with her fiery temper, laughing as flames consumed everything in her path. By eighteen years old, she had become feared by the woodland people. Her curse of slumber left her trapped in the same thorny prison she was put into. No prince arrived to save her. Thorns grew thick around her, a testament to her wild spirit. There she remained, a girl lost to her fury, forever entangled in the chaos she had created.

Ella Thomas (15)
The Peterborough School, Peterborough

The Lords Of The Skies

Stars filled the inky black sky, illuminating the details of the universe. Gods the size of galaxies hurled stars across the cosmos, smashing into quasars, causing ripples in the fabric of time and space.

Plubonious, the lord of the sky, gazed up at the spectacle of the universe's creation. "Someday, I shall own those galaxies."

"I will rot here along with the bugs and beetles," said Helldromibys, the lord of the earth. "It is simply my fate."

"Fate is simply an anchor. I shall fly," said Plubonious as he climbed into space, revealing to Helldromibys the beauty of the universe.

"Faith?"

Toby McGowan (12)
The Royal Ballet School, Richmond Park

Hansel And Gretel: The Truth Revealed

The esteemed Hansel and Gretel escaped near death thanks to their quick thinking... or did they? Were they really smart and quick-witted? From my perch on the branch, I'll reveal the truth.

Hansel and Gretel strode into the woods after curfew. They dropped breadcrumbs, but they dissolved without them noticing. They discovered a house smothered in mouthwatering sweets. I cawed immediately, three times, warning the two. Their curiosity controlled them. Brainwashed, they were lured into the house... and... they're no longer alive.

Little did they know that there were several warnings that they chose to ignore, and the consequences showed.

Yoshino Harding (11)
The Royal Ballet School, Richmond Park

The Twisted Slipper

Cinderella's fairy godmother sent her to the ball with a warning, "Magic is never kind." But she didn't listen. The prince was mesmerised, dancing only with her. Yet, with each step, the glass slippers tightened, biting into her skin. When the clock struck twelve, she tried to run - but the shoes didn't let her. Agony surged as the glass twisted, fusing to her bones. She fell, gasping as her gown unravelled and her body stiffened.
From the shadows, her godmother smiled. "You wished for a new life," she whispered. "Now you're trapped in it forever." And the fairy godmother disappeared.

Orla Warren (12)
The Royal Ballet School, Richmond Park

Little Red: Good Girl? No!

Little Red Riding Hood was known for her playful and mischievous ways, always seeking adventure.
One day, as she ventured through the woods, she crossed paths with the town's prime minister. Feeling rebellious, she decided to play a trick - only it went too far. She accidentally maimed him severely, and he had to be rushed to the hospital. The town was in shock, whispering about what had happened.
Red, feeling guilty, realised the consequences of her actions. From that day on, Little Red regretted her actions. That day, her mother forced Little Red to go to her grandmother.
Don't be naughty.

Collins Rodrigues-Hesketh (11)
The Royal Ballet School, Richmond Park

Hotel Burchianti

Mia and Alberto were excited about their holiday in Italy, eagerly checking into their charming hotel. As they entered the lobby, the receptionist complimented Mia, saying, "I like your eyes." It felt strange, but they brushed it off.

Later that night, the couple heard footsteps approaching their room. Hearts racing, they quickly fled and hid in the attic. As they caught their breath, their eyes widened in horror at the sight before them - an array of old, lifelike dolls, staring back.

The air grew cold, and a sinister presence filled the space. Mia touched a doll, and transformed into one.

Milan Yep (12)

The Royal Ballet School, Richmond Park

What If?

One day, as Cindy and her mum were walking through the park, a gigantic tree slowly started to tilt. Noticing this, Cindy pulled her mother away, saving her life. "Woah!" said her mum. "I almost died. But you saved me."
"I couldn't let you die!"
That Christmas, Cindy and her mother went to meet up with her stepmom and her three ugly stepsisters. Her stepmum seemed nice, but she did catch her scowling at her mother a few times.
Suddenly, everything went black. The last thing Cindy saw was her grinning mother. "Goodbye, Cinderella. *Mwahahaha!*"

Charlie Waller (11)
The Royal Ballet School, Richmond Park

The Vritra Prince

My heart trembled as the lustrous golden door unlocked. Astonished by the peculiar sight before my eyes, I ambled closer to what seemed like a... frog? Royal members of my family scurried up behind me, gleaming. A prudent Hindu priest commenced an unusual ceremony in which I was to be married! Little did they know, myself and this... frog planned this for years.

Steadily, I moved closer towards the frog and... *Boom!* I morphed into a Vritra in one's good time! Citizens astonishingly evacuated the building despite the fact that I was bound to blow the village up in three... two...

Nylah Ali (12)
The Royal Ballet School, Richmond Park

Checkmate, Your Majesty

She tried to escape Wonderland; she really did, but deep down, Alice knew something was holding her back.

The Queen of Hearts laughed and said, "I will make sure you never escape." So Alice stopped trying. She learned the rules and twisted them like the Cheshire Cat's grin.

One by one, the court fell - pawn to knight, knight to queen. When Alice finally sat upon the throne, the Queen of Hearts knelt before her, trembling. "Off with her head!" Alice laughed, and just like that, Wonderland had a new queen. And this time, they all knew she wasn't leaving.

Tilly Thomas (13)
The Royal Ballet School, Richmond Park

Betrayal

Shock, utter shock, pulsed through my veins, my mind churning and throbbing with confusion. *How is this possible?* Thoughts dashed through my mind. *I must be dreaming, it's not true.* A shock of realisation busted down my spine. Magic was real and I was the one to find it, hand in hand with my best friend, the most trustworthy person I know.

I looked behind me and saw something so shocking that I had to double-take. It was my friend pointing a gun at my head. "Do it," I said, "just do it. I love and have faith. You must have reasoning."

Frankie Keita (12)

The Royal Ballet School, Richmond Park

Riding Hood

Lightning struck. Thunder roared. Hail poured. Little Red Riding Hood knocked on her grandmother's door. No one answered. She knocked again. Still, no answer. She went in.

The door creaked. As she slowly opened the door, the floorboards rasped as she walked, and a gust of wind hit her like a ghost. She walked further and deeper into the amorphous cottage. She called for her grandmother, but there was no answer until moments later.

A shadow of a creature slowly emerged behind her. It was a wolf. She walked backwards. She hit the wall. She was never ever seen again.

Eliana Tse (13)
The Royal Ballet School, Richmond Park

The Seven Deadly Dwarfs

As her pale face lay unmoving in the moonlight, I realised how much power I had... We trusted the queen, but as the days had gone by, I had watched the others glare at her; greed and betrayal growing in their misty, unrecognisable eyes. My realisation sank in: I would carry this burden forever.

As I gazed at myself in the mirror, it smiled slyly and muttered, "You are the best of them all." The words spread through me like poison, infecting me with bloodthirsty power.

Snatching up the deadly vial, I tipped it cunningly into Snow's soft, innocent lips.

Felicity Ward (11)

The Royal Ballet School, Richmond Park

Untitled

In a dark forest, Hansel and Gretel wandered, lost and hungry. They stumbled upon a candy-coated house, its sugary surface glistening under the moonlight.
Drawn in by the sweet aroma, they entered, only to find that inside was a trap. The witch with hollow eyes and a wicked grin welcomed them with open arms. But as they feasted, the walls whispered secrets of her past victims.
When they tried to escape, the door vanished, sealing their fate. The next morning, the forest was silent, save for the sound of crunching on bones as the witch prepared for her next meal.

Joseph Phillips (13)
The Royal Ballet School, Richmond Park

The Deadly Duckling

One day, in the meadows by a stream, a duckling was born with six other cute ducks, but this duckling was different. It was bigger, red-eyed, and smelly. The other ducklings bullied him for his looks. The other ducks' actions changed him and made him even bigger, with even brighter red eyes.

As he grew up with the other ducks, they stopped growing, but he didn't. He never stopped until one day, he had had enough of the other ducks bullying him and decided to take charge.

The next day, he woke up, and ate all six ducklings, and lived happily ever after.

Ned Phillips (12)
The Royal Ballet School, Richmond Park

Wake Up

The cold air brushed past my arm as I hesitated to go through the huge, dark-brown oak doors. "Come on, or are you a chicken?" said Sarah. Everyone started laughing at me, so I pushed in front of them and went in.

Bang! The doors slammed shut. I quickly tried to open the doors, but it wasn't working. I suddenly heard screaming, but then there was nothing. I started to cry and hoped it was a dream.

"Wake up! Wake up!" I whispered to myself. I then felt a cold presence behind me. I froze in place. "Please be a dream!"

Uzziah Gray (12)
The Royal Ballet School, Richmond Park

Freedom

The towering walls suffocated me, driving me insane every passing day. The rats became my friends and the floor my bed. But, very often, you would be able to see a snarling beast, with piercing blue eyes and wild hair, lurking deep beneath the shadows.

As time blurred, I became a prisoner to my own mind. I was consumed by hunger and madness! I'd lost my mind!

As I lay in despair, the lock clicked. Finally! The doors creaked open... A sea of colourful hills and happiness greeted me! But as I glanced back, there I lay. Soundly asleep. Motionless...

Rosie Zhang (11)
The Royal Ballet School, Richmond Park

Untitled

Hansel and his sister Gretel realise their stepmother has abandoned them in the woods. They search the area and find a house made of gingerbread. Excitedly, they run and knock on the door.

An old lady answers and invites them in, giving them some delicious homemade sweets. She goes to the oven to get some fresh gingerbread for them, but the greedy children push her in and turn up the heat. They laugh and feast for hours on all the treats.

Suddenly, the house catches fire. They flee for their lives, but they're too fat to get out the door!

Arlo Hooper (12)

The Royal Ballet School, Richmond Park

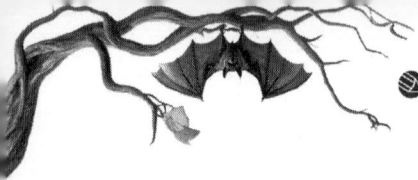

Once Upon A Nightmare

My sixteenth birthday was coming up. I woke up from a terrible nightmare. It was saying things like the generation was going to be horrid, and I wasn't going to get the same happy ending as my mother. I didn't even believe this nonsense anyway.

I headed down to breakfast, not caring about the warnings that had been given to me. Just as I was putting the handmade apple pie in my mouth, I felt a spiky feeling. I slowly took it out. Then, *gasp*, it was a beautiful, deadly, poisonous rose. I accidentally pricked my finger.

Yixin Zhou (12)
The Royal Ballet School, Richmond Park

Belle's Remorse

A thin layer of frigid air roamed around my surroundings. Scar's blood trailed through my arm, drenching me in red liquid. My black cloak embraced me. His fanged teeth seemed like a distant memory. Did I mean anything to him? Was he just making the most of his prisoner? All the memories we had twirling my yellow dress, him throwing down his soup. I really thought he was a true prince. It turned out I was wrong. He was a beast.

Papa says to never judge a book by its cover. I listened to him and I wholeheartedly regret it.

Ariella Assulin (11)
The Royal Ballet School, Richmond Park

The Wings Of Icarus After Death

Icarus fell into the sea, but this was not the end. Something stirred, born of regret. Daedalus had crafted the wings, but not all of his creations were meant for flying. The labyrinth hid a darker secret. Icarus rose from the depths, eyes ablaze. The sun had taken Icarus, but now it was time for him to rise. The night grew thick with unnatural heat. The stars flickered in fear, limning his cloak.

Oliver Quinn (11)
The Royal Ballet School, Richmond Park

Untitled

Once upon a time, Rumpelstiltskin was standing outside the village hall. "Let me in, let me in!" Rumpelstiltskin shouted, "I'm hungry for children!" *Knock, knock, knock.*
"We aren't gonna let you eat our kids!" one of the mums said.
"Fine, then I'll do it the hard way!" Rumpelstiltskin shouted down, climbing down the chimney. *Bang!* Rumpelstiltskin fell down the chimney. "I will give you ten seconds to bring me the children, or I will eat you all!"
"We won't let you eat them!" everyone shouted.
"One, two, three, four, five, six, seven, eight, nine, ten! It's dinnertime, everyone!"

Joe Tamblin (14)
Torpoint Community College, Torpoint

Beauty And The Beast

Belle and the Beast were dancing in the ballroom. Belle held the Beast close and whispered, "Lights out for you, you gullible mutt."
Bang. A cage dropped over the Beast as he looked at Belle with disappointed eyes. "I thought you were different."
"Well, you thought wrong," replied Belle. She opened the doors and shouted, "Go get him, boys!"
A large crowd flowed into the ballroom. They were carrying all kinds of weapons, and soon Belle was on her knees, watching the crowd.
Men dissected the trusting Beast. By dawn, there was nothing left but horns and rushing maroon blood.

Phoebe Danson (11)
Torpoint Community College, Torpoint

Too Perfect

I set my eyes on the land of Oz. "Where's your shoes?" I spun around, a scarecrow? "Sorry, I am confused, I don't have a brain." A man of metal jumped out. "And I don't have a heart!"
"I don't have courage." A nervous lion appeared.
"We will take you to Oz! Take these ruby heels." Taken aback, I followed.
"Thank you all," I praised. "You are too perfect."
"What?"
"Too perfect."
"We need a heart, brain, and bravery." I gasped; I tried to run, but it was too late. I lay in a pool of my blood.

Myrtille Gibbs (12)
Torpoint Community College, Torpoint

The Labyrinth

He woke in a dingy corridor made of ancient stone and vines. "Where am I?" he said, confused and worried. "Where am I?" he shouted.

He ran down the winding corridor to escape. He stopped, there were two corridors. Left or right. One to safety and one to go deeper. He had to choose.

"Wait, what's that?" There were banging noises coming from the right. There, sprinting towards him, was a half-bull, half-man. "What the-"

Boom! It knocked him to the floor, breaking his shoulder completely. He tried to stand but couldn't. All he could see was his doom.

Tristan Hill (12)

Torpoint Community College, Torpoint

Mack And The Beanstalk

Mack walks back from the bank, realising he is broke, with Peypa Pig depressed and upset. All of a sudden, he comes across a magic trader. "Hello, young man." "Hello. My name is Mack, and this is Peypa." The trader looks around his stall.

"I could trade Peypa for some magic beans," he laughs evilly, then coughs. "Sorry, sore throat." *Click*. He disappears with Peypa. Mack gets home and plants the bean, hoping it will grow.

He wakes up the next morning and - *boom!* There is a ginormous hole in his garden. He climbs down, never to be seen again.

Freddie Shilton (12)
Torpoint Community College, Torpoint

The Death Of Astroe

"They've rotated the land without me!" I looked outside the window. "Great." During the rotation, the land of the Twisteds had spun here. It was the opposite of the fairyland.

Rap-tat! "The Twisteds are here..." Worst of all, it was my twin, Evil Astroe. "I've got to escape!" I knew this day would come; I had an escape hatch at the back. I pulled the lever and jumped down, but evil Betty was waiting for me. She looked normal, but her spine was pushed out of her body. She looked at me; I couldn't move. She swiped at me. I exploded...

Mikey Bright (13)

Torpoint Community College, Torpoint

The Real Dream

Tick, tock, tick, tock. All that I could hear was that clock. Not knowing what time it was, but the moon still stared into my bedroom. I closed my eyes, all noises eventually disappearing. Silence.
I wish I could say it was a dream, but I honestly don't know if it was real. I saw it, just there. I wasn't sure what it was, but it looked at me, calling me, telling me to come closer. I was in a forest. The trees danced with the wind.
Boom! I spun around, nothing. *Where's it gone? What had been calling me? I'm dreaming...*

Isla Symons-Goncalves (12)
Torpoint Community College, Torpoint

Untitled

The water suddenly bubbled and screeched like it was boiling. Long, purple tentacles shot into the sky and caught onto the ship. A Kraken! Men fell overboard as others prayed in the commotion. The captain, Pegleg, was flung off the ship into the burning sea. Soon, one man was left, Scratchface. The most feared man in the sea, he single-handedly fought off the Kraken. The Kraken sank back into the ocean, and Scratchface sailed back to shore.

Ten years later, Scratchface captained his own crew, everything was going great until the water bubbled and screeched again...

Joe Davey (12)
Torpoint Community College, Torpoint

The Miner's Nightmare

One day, Larry was sitting at the end of the mine eating his delicious pasty. Today, he was particularly hungry, but so were the knockers. Larry didn't leave the knockers the end of his pasty like he usually did. His two brothers, Barry and Garry, warned him about this, but Larry ignored them.

During his next hours of work, Larry felt very sleepy and forgot that he had to be careful with the explosives.

The next day, Barry and Garry found a chewed-up, bloody Larry lying on the dirty floor surrounded by the knockers.

Miners! You've been warned!

Libby Weeks (12)
Torpoint Community College, Torpoint

Untitled

It's 6am. "Time to get up!" Mum calls out. I spring up from my bed and zoom downstairs.
"I'm so excited for my sleepover today!" I shout with so much energy that I could run a marathon. I sprint out the door, feeling the joy inside me wanting to burst out. I run and run and run until I can't anymore, and I finally reach his house. I knock on the door, but there is no answer. "That's strange," I say to myself. "He said this exact time." I open my coat pocket and grab my phone... It's Monday!

Aimee-Grace Ginger (13)
Torpoint Community College, Torpoint

Black Night

The glaring moonlight seeped through my eyelids,
waking me up. I was cold. The heat from my friends
was no longer keeping me warm. In fact, where were
they?
A shiver crawled down my back. Shaking, I unzipped
the tent door. The sound of the plastic rustling was the
only sound to be heard.
My eyes wandered. Letting out a deafening scream, my
gaze settled on a sack sitting in front of my knees. A
sack of bright red eyes and nose. My friends!
Still screaming, I felt a tight grasp grab my face.
Excruciating pain spread around my body.

Nell Staniforth (13)
Torpoint Community College, Torpoint

The Blind Ghost

A long time ago, there was a blind ghost. His dying wish was to see, but it was not fulfilled. Vengeful, he set off.

One night, the blind ghost found a spellbook leaning against a tree. Flicking through the pages, he found a spell for farsight - to see with another thing's eyes. He cackled softly. Waving his hands, he created a curse to force the living to carve faces into vegetables. Through their eyes, he could see.

And so, every year, when his spell is renewed, we carve our pumpkins... The blind ghost can watch us at last.

Isla-pearl Taylor (13)

Torpoint Community College, Torpoint

The Dead Pirates' Cave

The story begins with a man collecting some treasure from a pirate ship near Main Beach. He would row the treasure to the mainland, where another group of pirates would buy it.

The man began to sail back to land, his boat bursting with treasure, when a storm hit. Lightning sliced through the sky like knives. Eventually, he got back to shore, gasping. He had to dump all the treasure in the sea to save himself.

The pirates were furious. The man pleaded for mercy, but the pirates bound him with rope and left him in a cave to drown.

Milo Smith (13)
Torpoint Community College, Torpoint

The Split

She was just picking berries, a harmless walk. The path split into three. Her blood ran cold. This was how the fairy tales ended. There was never a happy ending. She was going to die out here, all alone, with no one to know.
She chose a path, the middle one. It was a safe choice, or so she thought.
Ianna was a small, nine-year-old girl who was just trying to pick berries for her mother, who was ill in bed. She was a kind girl, a girl who helped anyone. But when she was faced with utter darkness, her mind spiralled...

Bessie Eastment (13)
Torpoint Community College, Torpoint

Shrek 5

Lord Farquaad was going to eat the Gingerbread Man, until Donkey and I came running in to stop him. Donkey rammed Farquaad off his chair and flung the dinner table into the ceiling as though he were a bull in a china shop. I pulled out my sword, and tried slicing the man's head off, but he was too fast for me to catch him.

Then, all of a sudden, Dragon came in and swallowed him whole. The Gingerbread Man thanked us for saving him, but really, I just saved him for a snack!

He was delicious, personally speaking!

Finn Kelly (14)

Torpoint Community College, Torpoint

Gingerlocks And The Daddy Kangaroo

I have just got home from a nice evening stroll with my wife and kids, but when I get home, what do I find? Our barbecued fruit salad all gone!

When I want to have a sit-down and read, all of our chairs are destroyed except for Johnny's! And I can see traces of crispy grass.

As I walk into the next room, I close my eyes as I was expecting to see a kitchen on fire, but when I open them, I see an orange blob on the floor! But then realise, they had cracked their head open.

Joshua Toby (12)
Torpoint Community College, Torpoint

Misunderstood

The giant is dead. No one knows his story, so I'm going to tell you.

As a child, the giant was small for his age. People would pick on him for it. He got so sick of it that he turned into a rebel. He would steal things and mess around.

One day, a teacher got mad and decided to set a trap. He got his prized golden egg and placed it on a leaf. The small giant saw it and ran for it.

He got the egg, but his weight made him fall. No one saw him ever again.

Nevaeah Roberts (14)
Torpoint Community College, Torpoint

Goldilocks

"Hello, Daddy Bear, is the porridge done?"

"Yes."

"But it's hot."

"Let's go on a walk."

"Oh no."

Everything was broken and smashed. Their upstairs beds were broken. Food gone, nothing was the same other than the porridge because someone was eating it.

A murderous smile, a killer's face, with a blood-red knife, sprinted out of the house with a silencing aura.

Rhys Hulm (12)

Torpoint Community College, Torpoint

Hansel Needs To Die

6pm. I just found out that Hansel and I are going to be killed. This is my chance. I've hated him since birth. The favourite. The best. This ends today.

7pm. The witch who is killing us knows I know her plan. She's killing 'us' tonight.

7:30pm. I'm leaving that rancid house now. Gotta take some sweets for the road though. I'm waiting outside until he dies.

8pm. I hear his cries. Goodbye, my brother.

Amelia Payne (11)
Torpoint Community College, Torpoint

Young Writers Information

We hope you have enjoyed reading this book – and that you will continue to in the coming years.

If you're a young writer who enjoys reading and creative writing, or the parent of an enthusiastic poet or story writer, do visit our website www.youngwriters.co.uk. Here you will find free competitions, workshops and games, as well as recommended reads, a poetry glossary and our blog.

If you would like to order further copies of this book, or any of our other titles, then please give us a call or visit **www.youngwriters.co.uk.**

Young Writers
Remus House
Coltsfoot Drive
Peterborough
PE2 9BF
(01733) 890066
info@youngwriters.co.uk

Join in the conversation!

 YoungWritersUK   YoungWritersCW   youngwriterscw
 youngwriterscw   youngwriterscw-uk

**Watch the video
trailer here**